Turbulence

Turbulence

Poems

Tony Reevy

Iris Press
Oak Ridge, Tennessee

Cover Photo by Alextov

Book Design by Robert B. Cumming, Jr.

Library of Congress Cataloging-in-Publication Data

Names: Reevy, Tony, author.
Title: Turbulence : poems / Tony Reevy.
Description: Oak Ridge, Tennessee : Iris Press, [2022] | Summary: "In Turbulence, poet and non-fiction author Tony Reevy looks at "family" in the United States through the lens of one family and its members' collective experiences over the last fifty years. The poems in the book explore major paradoxes about the U.S.—a love of nature combined with environmental destruction; a democracy that for years denied the rights of millions; a wealthy country that offers little or no assistance for many of its people—and how they affect one extended family. Most importantly, Turbulence asks how families cope with such unexpected events as the death of a child, or a young mother or father—tragedies that our society largely chooses to ignore"— Provided by publisher.
Identifiers: LCCN 2022008679 (print) | LCCN 2022008680 (ebook) | ISBN 9781604542653 (paperback) | ISBN 9781604548198 (ebook)
Subjects: LCGFT: Poetry.
Classification: LCC PS3618.E4459 T87 2022 (print) | LCC PS3618.E4459 (ebook) | DDC 811/.6—dc23
LC record available at https://lccn.loc.gov/2022008679
LC ebook record available at https://lccn.loc.gov/2022008680

Acknowledgements

The author would also like to acknowledge the following publications where a number of these poems first appeared:

"After the Memorial," "Memory Care," "One Day After the Funeral," "Revenant," *The Awakenings Review;* "Water's Edge, Bear Mountain State Park," *Crab Orchard Review;* "At the Selma Amtrak Depot," "The Last House," *Earth's Daughters;* "At the Childhood Home," in Shirley Richburg, editor, *Familiar* (Baltimore: The People's Press, 2005); "Lightning in Wartime," "The Chief's Grave," *Lightning in Wartime* (Georgetown, Kentucky: Finishing Line Press, 2007); "Eno Hike, Three Weeks After the Death of a Friend," "Fall Evening, Harpers Ferry (1989)," *Magdalena* (Columbus, Ohio: Pudding House Publications, 2004); "Drive By," *Medical Literary Messenger;* "Child-Sitting," "Days" "Kepone Days," "These Hands," *Negative Capability Press* (website); "At the Crossroads," in *Of Burgers and Barrooms* (Charlotte: Main Street Rag Publishing, 2017); "The Millennium Holder," *pacificREVIEW;* "Northern Lights, Southern Town," *The Blotter;* "The Passengers," *Deronda Review;* "At Diamond Hill Cemetery," "Looking for Diamonds," *The Kerf;* "Amerika," *The Pedestal Magazine;* "Buckle Up," in Kenneth Salzmann and Sandi Gelles-Cole, editors, *What Remains* (Woodstock, New York: Gelles-Cole Literary Enterprises, 2018).

Thank you to my family, Caroline, Lindley and Ian, for their patience and support. And, as always, thank you to my poetry group—Bart, Maria and Morrow. Eric Weil and Maria Rouphail reviewed the manuscript—many thanks for their time, and their advice.

In memoriam: Katie Anderson

✈

Something sinister in the tone
Told me my secret must be known;
Word I was in the house alone
Somehow must have gotten abroad,
Word I was in my life alone,
Word I had no one left but God.

—Robert Frost, "Bereft"

Contents

Three

Four

Prelude

Kepone Days

We'd throw down our bikes—
just graduated from banana
seats to ten-speeds—at the end
of the squat row of new houses.

A broad flood-plain bank,
littered with Hurricane Agnes'
leavings, was our front porch
to the James.

Jordan's Point, the looming
bridge towers, just upstream.
Then, farther west, Hopewell
and its fuming chemical factories.

While we splashed, played—weekends
mostly—men labored in the old
filling station, which Allied Chemical
said it *didn't own*. And the plume spread

downstream towards us. Each Monday,
we'd go back to junior high together,
wearing our Converses,
if the river water soaking them
had dried.

Fall Evening, Harper's Ferry

1989

The headlight leaves us,
lights the tunnel,
crosses the Potomac,
and is gone.

Steps, rock-hewn
to the church.
The Jefferson Stone,
the hill-top
above us;
two black rivers below.

Rush of water;
velvet darkness
of sky blocked by mountains.
A screech and a bellow:
another train follows the first.

After it passes,
the cold night is silent.
Church-landing slates
chill through my shoes.
You, in your wool coat,
stand close, and warm.

Gripping my hand;
sharing the words
of our fifty-year dream.

Amerika

The packed island,
great, smoking train,
rust-red tipple.

Twenty years on,
the war, an oath,
a paper.

The grasping call
of a land
so vast, so wide.

Duck and cover,
they tell the kids,
duck and cover.

How came
this sudden retirement
by a great ocean?

Who knows the end?
Who can tell me
how this ends?

Eno Hike, Three Weeks After the Death of a Friend

Summer air sweet and thick,
forest damp and green.
Ground, where it shows, red.
In the clearing, verdant,
almost overgrown, sumac berries—
carmine, plump—show promise.

This path runs down the slope.
At its foot, the Eno flows
clear and even, but not too full.
You could walk across the rocks
now, no trouble, to the trail
on the other side.

I turn the bend and hike along
the river. Slow; time
to think. Suddenly, thunder—deep,
rolling—like a night phone call
bringing bad news. The breeze
stills.

Thunder means lightning.
In my dreams, I always die that way.

I quicken my pace; lose my thoughts.
Now, I see the whitened tree
like polished bone: a deadfall
rotting two years and waiting
to tumble.

Crossing the bridge, I hear
thrashing below. The commotion
resolves: sun-bathing copperhead,
frightened by my walk,
coiling to strike.

It's three feet under and five
to my right; faced away
from the path. But it
could have been along
the trail, sunning, unseen.

I hurry to the car,
a refuge from lightning
and snakes, parked away
from deadfalls. I've never
seen them on this path before.

At the Childhood Home

To the Krakauer family, in sympathy

She came back over
spring break. Lay down
one night, wearing
her flannel pajamas—
a relic of childhood—
with a glass of water
and a bottle of pills.

How to describe
a mother, in the morning,
finding her daughter cold,
stiff, sightless. Gone.
Gone to where no one
believes children go.
Not first.

One

Lost

I forgot the camera
on this beach trip—
photos of children
with friends, parents,
grandparents
lost
before they even
exist.

Caroline forgot
the special bottle of wine
set aside for romance
in our room
away from the kids.

The kids forgot
their beach buckets,
shovels, rakes—
the Ben Franklin
has plenty more.

And now, today, Granddaddy
doesn't remember
his son.

Water's Edge, Bear Mountain State Park

The cast-concrete landing
where Day Liners tied up
at the end of the trail
and road. A few bloated shad
bob at its side—
the Hudson eases by.
A stick-thin man dips string
tied to chicken necks
in brown water.
The air smells of fish—
not unpleasant—
and summer forest.

Our daughter runs
up and down the ramp,
hears scrabbling
against plastic, races
to the white painter's bucket
full of tiny crabs,
peers inside. A knife
lies at her feet.
I reach for her hand,
the fisherman scrambles over,
whisper-screams as if
gripped by the throat.

Later, Lindley asks
why the man screamed—
maybe because
his crabs were
too small—and why
he whispered—*he might*
be sick. Why
did he have the knife—
to cut up his bait.
For a minute, gripped
in her car seat behind us,
she is silent.

The Pottery Fish

My daughter dropped
the pottery fish
her grandmother made.

Yellow and green, white
clay showing where
scales, fins were scribed.

She brought it to me
in two pieces—and,
as she showed me,

dropped it again.
Bad girl, I snapped—
I can see a day

when Grandmommy
will shape no more fish
for her, for me.

That hurt look. How love
tells us, begs us,
to forgo our passionate

judgments. Next
morning, I glued
the shards. After

they held, I put the fish
at her place on our table
before she woke up.

The Chief's Grave

One who tries but fails—
Junaluska's—last home
is a rise in Robbinsville
just bought back
by the tribe. We stopped
to pay our respects,
my boy and I walked
the medicine trail.

The grave was fenced,
filled with flowers.
Ian didn't want to leave,
clung to the enclosure,
threw his shoe inside.
Cursing, too low—I hope—
for him to hear, praying
people in the museum
couldn't see, I jumped
the rail, got it back.

You never know—you
never know—what
a boy's going to do, where
a boy's going to take you.

Submarine, Inner Harbor, Baltimore

This long, thin cylinder
of the depths, with only
a few inches of steel
between the crew
and death by breathing,
gulping black water
instead of fetid air.

Skeletons, my son
says, *skeletons*, as he
screams, scrambles
down the corridor,
through the hatches
to the light.

Lightning in Wartime

The storms have hit
every night this week.
A white flash—this is the
first year I've compared
bolts to phosphorus
bombs—and, in five seconds,
the knell of thunder.
I get up, turn off the
computer, a loose caulked
window rattles—there's
always something—one
of my children wakes.

The night cooling of thick
summer air makes the show,
they say. Not men,
not the turn of A-10's off
a run over Piedmont trees
instead of jungle, desert, the
jagged, broken rocks of Khyber.

At the Craft Store

Becca's mom died
this morning,
my daughter says,
and I cried
at lunch time.

She skips to the stuffed
animal display
while I think over
next week, try
to fit in the funeral,

make a note
on scrap paper:
get stamps and a card
for the husband, three
young daughters
left motherless

and pocket it
as my daughter hands
me *Lucy's birthday*
present, and can I get
a ball of yarn, and these
new scissors?

Somewhere on I-79, Between Pittsburgh and Clarksburg

This compact car, filled
with those I love most,
brakes down the steep slope.

Fog-bound orbs float
by—massive streetlights,
truck, pickup headlights.
Our lamps barely cut
the damp dark.

*Let us reach our hotel
safely, soon. Let us avoid
the charging, metal
monoliths of this mountain
highway night.*

Soundside

End of the sandbank,
Roanoke—flat calm.
Ian paces a beeline
to shore, I follow.
At a distance,
it seems he's walking
on water.
Reaches the edge

before I get there—
a ten-year-old proud
to beat Dad. He picks up
his shoes, we cross
the dunes together
towards home.

Two

The Millennium Holder

In the morning, my son
talked about the Millennium
Holder—a place bigger
than the universe,

where everyone has a double.
*If you're a policeman
here, then you're a robber
in the Holder.*

At his grandfather's house,
my son doesn't want to go
in. He plays in the road,
riding a scooter, dodging

periodic passing cars.
Inside, his Granddaddy,
brain shrinking, wanders,
a ghost before his time.

The Passengers[1]

We're on the new train—
it's pushing limits, barreling
west through Southside.

Sun's up. Through the coach
window, U S 460's blacktop
appears, vanishes
on the other side
of new-growth scrub.

Too soon, we roar under
the new bypass—and I've missed
seeing my old school.
Maybe its run-down
brick husk
is gone—

the place where I used to sit and watch
the freights, endless conveyors
of coal, never dreaming—
What were my dreams then?—

that, grown, I'd journey by,
my son sitting next to me,
watching, laughing, today.

Jamestown Ruins

It's cold, bitter cold
as Ian and I wander
the grounds.

Low brick walls
all that remain
of these lost lives.

Hundreds gone
in the starving time—

and street women
shipped here in boatloads
as "wives."

*Be fruitful
and multiply.*

My son sees,
in mind's eye,
cannon turned
on the church—

its tower the last
survivor. I tell
him of Bacon's war.

And Ian says
he sees men, women
approaching us:

Striding ahead, but their feet
are not touching
the ground.

Turbulence

It's a big plane
for a domestic flight
but the wild wind
bats it
like a cat pawing
butterflies
to the ground.

And the ground now sounds
like a good place to be.

Below, in the transplant ward,
my niece, just admitted, tosses,
unsteady—dreams, body failing,
blood, marrow oozing
with errant cells.

She can't see our contrail,
doesn't notice the faint
hum overhead.

To the Funeral

In memoriam, John F. Weaver, Sr., 1930-2013

The take-out lunch is packed—
we're ready
to go. The train blares
its arrival.
But we are traveling
to view one
who has already departed
and lies preserved

for the prodigals to see—
while the faithful,
like those on this journey,
wound themselves. We board
the coach, another whistle,
and we clatter away.

Drive By

I'm on I-95, southbound—
bulk of the hospital
looming on my right,
so close.

It's illegal, I tell
myself, *to use this car
for a personal visit.*

But I don't really want
to stop. A traveler, after
a long journey, seeing
this fellow traveler, close
to the end of her road—
it would be too much.

I grip the wheel harder,
tap the accelerator,
set the cruise control
a bit higher,
drive on.

Looking for Diamonds

A great place to find gemstones,
we were told.
My son runs up the slope,
I trudge behind.

Sign: DIAMOND HILL
CEMETERY.
*The man didn't mention
a graveyard*, I say.

Low wind rises,
rattles the last tree-
bound leaves.

Up the path, Ian's foot
catches on a stone.

Then, we see them
all around us, mounded
under autumn's fallen ones.

*This was for slaves,
Ian—these stones
are grave markers.*

> *But they are just rocks,
> Daddy.*

At the Selma Amtrak Depot

The long visit is over—
we're at the station,
day before Christmas Eve,
waiting room crowded,
frantic with children.

The old ones
pay them no mind—
lost in worries
about their journey.

I can't stop thinking
about time spent
in the hospital.

I look up, through
the platform window.

My son stands silent,
framed by wood, glass,
staring straight at me.

For a moment, I think
I'm looking a mirror—

and that it's me there,
trying to understand,
waiting for a train.

Hospital Prom

The gowns are traditional
and the Society
lent wigs.

But these teens
don't have dates.

And stolen kisses
could be fatal.

Katie can't come—
hers came back.

We guess she will leave
the hospital
for good
soon.

The band starts up again,
and those that can,
dance.

The wallflowers—the unsteady
ones, those pulling IV carts—
watch from the sidelines.

Calling

Tap-click of static
on the land line,
no voice.

Neither party
can find words.

The news—a child
is dying.

What is there to say
when all you can do
is listen?

Child-Sitting

Her hand is warm,
the respirator's
gasp-rasp-click
louder than the snap
of the quartz clock.
Outside, a fresh Spring
forces buds to open
under a blank window.

The machine's sighs
tell the time here,
less than a day
until they
turn it
off.

After the Memorial

Snow falling fast, so fast.
The day's events
are done: siblings
say goodbye, disunite
again. The car is warm, but outside
the worst, late storm of the year.
Hard to concentrate;
I grip the wheel.

Back home—they went
on ahead—live
those who need me
to get up
rather than stay in
for a long, long sleep.

One Day after the Funeral

The cooling engine ticks
and sighs as I wait,
encased in this metal box.

The bell rings, doors open,
a trickle, a stream,
of young ones.

Then, the short, slim figure—
far away but I'd recognize
her anywhere.

Lindley walks towards me,
opens the door,
settles in quietly.

How was your day?

I don't know.

I start the car, pull away,
we ride home
in silence.

Three

In the child's room

there's no dust,
vacuum cleaner marks
on the floor.

The door's pulled
almost all the way
shut—

Her cat doesn't come
in for company
anymore.

There's no laundry
in the hamper.

A stainless canister
on her dresser
reflects the light.

Outside, a new sun
raises mist
from the frosted lawn.

At the Crossroads[2]

Two US highways—49, 61—
off the interstates,
overhung by a fancy
sign: crossed guitars.

Rain gushes down.
My son and I shelter
under golf umbrellas—
my wife jockeys
to keep
the Nikon dry.

A wizened woman
ambles up from somewhere,
nowhere. *I's
a miracle*—she points
to the puckered trach hole
in her throat.

*Have twenty dollars;
feed my babies?*

I hand her a five.

My son turns, stares
as she crosses Highway 61,
disappears through mist
into the Bojangles'.

Pilgrimage

Wind rushes in the pines—
sounds like a river,
but no broad waters lap
this old mill town.

Up the access road,
past the Betts mausoleum,
a curve, then a row
of monuments.

The American Legion
finally installed a plaque.

His tour of duty
took him to Russia, Turkey,
but the ashes lie here,
beyond time,
the Cold War,
the wild Washington years.

The brass plate reads,
"Sergeant, Air Force"—

I shiver in the spring chill
pull my jacket close,
learning that life
is remembered
with a short summary.

The Last House

The movers, salvage men
are gone,
what was alive
echoes.

Strange how large
thirteen-hundred square feet
can look
when empty.

Close the garage,
put the control
in a bag
with the keys.

The door rattles down,
clunks the concrete.

Turn away.

The only near sound
my footsteps
on the driveway concrete,
a beep-beep
as the remote
unlocks my car.

these hands

once spattered with slip
or clay

smooth no more
shape no more
coil and throw no more

but they're not
quietly folded

they're rubbing together
restless as if they—
or something—
need to be washed

In Memoriam

Katie Anderson

The green heat
doesn't feel like May.

Volunteers, family
set up a memorial
on the folding table—
mostly photos, leukemia
wristband, laminated poster.

Friends talk about graduation,
college choices.

A breeze stalks
the fresh-mown lawn,
brings a whiff
of parked cars.

The poster flaps, flies.

I rush for it, tape it leeward
to a convenient
chain-link fence.

It will hold there,
as long as the wind
is with us.

Revenant

I am a ghost,
walking in shadows.

Less real than the ones
who are gone.

Less sure than the electorate
in November.

With less faith than the members
of a New Covenant Church.

Choking on a native language,
but avoiding fast food.

A crow calls—
there's no answer.

And I don't answer.

A gutter leaks, drips loudly,
and the wind chime
mutters once,
just once.

Days

Time—
photo-frozen
in the smiles.

Today, some growing,
some gone—
from home,
or forever.

Place the print,
close the cover,
scan the image,
hit *save*.

The Call

Tonight, the stars
seem like pinpricks
in a sheet
of black rubber.

And the road
a cracked relic
made of tar
and crushed pebbles.

The phone rings
and rings
and no one answers.

Won't someone pick up,
before this continued
tintinnabulation
claims me?

Yesterday, when I walked
my favorite trail,
the plants were yellowed
and the creek
had run dry.

At Diamond Hill Cemetery

Violets along the trail—
first green of spring.
Purple, smallish blooms,
new heart-leaves.

Stones, under last year's mold,
mound the site.

A sign admonishes,
Respect the fallen.

Two trees, grown together,
rub with the wind.

At the end of the path,
cradled in crotch
of tree roots, flat rocks
marked with messages.

Some about old times,
Bondage, lost years.
Others contemporary,
Dead at five, OD.

And, at bottom left
of the pile, *Cancer.*

A breeze sweeps past;
the joined cedar, white oak,
creak, cry together.

Bluets

White bells
ringing in the first warm
week of March.

A bookmark—
like leaf-fall ushering
in winter's chill.

Three Marches ago,
diagnosis. Two Marches
ago, an end.

Last March, the struggle
to accept,
and the pills.

This year, I find
I no longer think
about it
all the time.

Only when reminded—
one never knows when

or how
that will happen,

simple blossoms
taking me back.

✈

Four

Passing the Cemetery in Ebensburg

On the way to the Sheetz,
where I plan to discharge
my bladder, buy the obligatory
Coke, this assemblage
of gravestones and grass
seems familiar.

Then I remember.
My grandmother and grandfather—
Pap and Mama, they were called—
are buried here.

Born in a far land,
they lie in this place,
nearest relations
now hundreds of miles away.

I never met them.

The county-seat cemetery
is vast. Should I look
for the graves?

I hit the brakes—a moment—
then I tap the accelerator
and drive on.

Memory Care

One who can see
all the world's evil
cannot sleep.

Must tell them—
get up, pain.

Walk the halls,
quiet, dark—
they are keeping
me here.

If I push this door,
the alarm brings
them, the black ones,
the group.

What to do?

Buying a Plot

For Dad, and Mom, Maplewood Cemetery

This is a good one,
Charlie says. *Below here,*
it gets too damp.

He waves the metal detector,
finds a hit.
His helper shovels out
the marker.

We'll put him on the left—
the man's side.
The side you stood on
when you got married.

A flight of Canada geese
crosses the sky,
blackbirds roost
in the trees.

I like it, I say,
and Charlie writes the order
on his list.

We get back in his truck,
drive towards the office.

Charlie stops along the way,
side of the access road.

My son's over there,
and this is my great-granddaughter.
A blessing—the doctors
said she'd never walk
or talk
if she lived.

There's a doll on the stone.

Working here, Charlie says,
*I get to see her
every day.*

The Next Job

Didn't expect to see
you here, Jerry.

       Yeah, it's busy
      right now.

After this, I have one
in Mechanicsville.
Someone you
don't know.

The two priests pause,
look at me.

I'm the son,
I say.

Okay, the taller,
heavier one says.

Your father—we'll
give him
a good send-off.

Telenovelas

The social-contact lounge
is crowded—
all seats taken.

The beautiful screen-people,
women caked in makeup,
all curvaceous, argue
in rapid-fire
Español.

Viewers pale-white,
listless, eyes turned
to the screen.

At a casual glance,
watching, listening.

No one
who lives here
speaks a word
of Spanish.

Lost to dreams,
soon to fall
asleep.

This is Hallowed Ground

Diamond Hill Cemetery, Berry Hill Plantation,
near South Boston, Virginia

the sign
says—and

Be respectful.

chiggers in the grass
short pants

should have
remembered

trees still
creak groan
together

next time
bring a stone

talisman
cairn

like the turf-
ridden rocks

surrounding me

bench sit
ask for guidance

hearing none

need to go

hurry back
onto the path
a woman walking asks

*Where did you
come from?*

Bells

Call the faithful
to mass.

Unexpected, they clang
out, then echo
from the stone walls.

Mother is dying.

The peals end.
Sun gleams
through morning mist;
a crow calls
to no one.

Buckle Up

The weight beside me
trips on the *passenger seat*
occupied indicator.

My car beeps,
the *seat belt*
unfastened light
blinks red.

In the faux marble
container, nothing
but "homogenized" dust.

Still, like the director
suggested, I wrap
the seatbelt around Mom—
her last ride—
and strap her in.

Holidays, After the Passing

The leaves have fallen;
they lie in bleaching piles.
Tree lots have sprung up,
it seems, from nowhere.
It's time to address cards,
buy gifts, plan returns home.
But home is here now—
the house where we grew up is gone.

She called us together
every year, mended hurt hearts
and torn shirts.

Blessed be the peacemakers,
blessed be those who keep us whole
for yet another year.

Walking the Eno trail

alone—
thinking about the past
few years.

Behind me, a twig
snaps, a foot-
fall.

I turn, look,
but there's no one
there.

Trapping Blues

The young woman
stuffing a mauled
bait fish
into the crab trap—

Can this be the baby
with curly hair
I walked in the stroller
every night?

The boat rocks,
the day-old dolphin—
Restaurants call it mahi-mahi,
the research associate says—
reeks of incipient rot.

Lindley finishes loading,
snaps the wire lid closed,
tosses float, trap
over the side.

The float bobs,
fluorescent pink
with a white band.

Off the port bow
a dolphin—the mammal,
not the fish—breaches,
then another,
and another.

River Year

The river flows with a slow-sluicing sound,
taking its well-worn mud-path to the sea.
Meeting Durham's harder-rock ledge, it swerves,
cuts a new way through less difficult ground.
In summer here, the still air smells of mold,
in fall, come softer leaf-steps on the trail.
In winter, there are brown tree skeletons,
then, the woodland turns again, to sudden green.

The years flow on to a twice-empty end,
sister, brother go under the scalpel.
Still the Eno flows, summer-sewage tinged,
makes its meander down to the ocean.
A river otter, the first here in years,
waits on the bank, whiskers twitching, for fish.

At the Eno, Close to Flood Stage

The path is damp,
the skies cloudy,
but not threatening.

The only sounds—
rush of water,
birds chittering,
planes overhead.

There's a touch
of leaf-dappled sun.

So, I go ahead,
farther and farther
from the safety-shell
of my car.

About halfway
through the loop,
sudden thunder.

It's far off
but not too far,
booming like
Dad's funeral salute.

I take a shortcut
back, up the hill,
past a father and two sons
just starting down.

I think of warning
them—life's lapping water,
sudden bolts—but don't,
leaving them to find
their own way.

number 13 dream

every night
I run down the tracks
past the reeking
boney piles
along a river
rising over its banks

so humid
the air is green

Thirteen Mine
is burning

coal-black smoke
licked by bright flames
boiling

and I don't want
to see

I don't want to
go back, Daddy,
I don't want
to go back

Northern Lights—Southern Town[3]

Under the glimmering arch
   of green-ghosted sky,
This shouldn't happen here, I told
   my daughter and son.

We stood stilled, watching.
As ions winked, swirled—emerald
   and red—we dreamed
of Alaska, Canada, and Mars.

Soon, too soon, aurora borealis
   was gone.

Leaving sky jaundiced
   by city lights,
their glow diminishing
   the stars.

Endnotes

1 On Amtrak Train 88, between Norfolk and Richmond, Virginia.

2 The crossroads in Clarksdale, Mississippi, where bluesman Robert Johnson reportedly sold his soul to the Devil so that he could play guitar like one possessed.

3 Aurora borealis, seen looking north down Virginia Avenue, Durham, North Carolina.

Tony Reevy is a graduate of North Carolina State University, UNC-Chapel Hill and Miami University. His previous publications include poetry, non-fiction, essays and short fiction, including the non-fiction books *Ghost Train!*, *O. Winston Link: Life Along the Line*, *The Railroad Photography of Jack Delano* and *The Railroad Photography of Lucius Beebe and Charles Clegg*; the poetry chapbooks *Green Cove Stop*, *Magdalena*, *Lightning in Wartime* and *In Mountain Lion Country*; and the full books of poetry, *Old North*, *Passage* and *Socorro*. He lives in Durham, North Carolina with wife, Caroline Weaver, and children Lindley and Ian.

www.ingramcontent.com/pod-product-compliance
Lightning Source LLC
Chambersburg PA
CBHW031402060726

47590CB00007B/2912